# Anthologies of Incompetence

Samantha Silverman

BookLeaf Publishing

India | USA | UK

Presentation by *BookLeaf Publishing*

Web: www.bookleafpub.com

E-mail: info@bookleafpub.com

ISBN: 9789363314184

First edition 2024

# ACKNOWLEDGEMENT

I want to acknowledge my dad for helping and supporting me in the publication on this book.

Love, your number one daughter 

Thanks to Abby Schneider & James Macklin for editing.

# Another Light

I thought I didn't know my worth before I met
you.
I wasn't a light, more like a broken strand of
parts trying to ignight.
Between cracked glass, missing bulbs, broken
pices, and tangled parts,
I wasn't sure I even worked right.
Then I met you and there was a spark.
Some call it love,
Some call it manipulation,
but I was in the dark.
A gaslight,
but I didn't listen.
Piece by piece each part of me started to
glisten.
I felt like I was being put back together.
You were my glue, holding true.
Bulbs were replaced, and again I started to glow
like new.
It's easy to look at a light and just see it shining.
Glue is only temporary,
for another you were pining.
My bulbs went out, broke, and while I was
trying my best to still sprout,
you confirmed my only doubt.

# A Different Forever

It is hard not to think about you, and all the
bullshit that we've been through.
The ups and downs,
the highs and lows
that's how ever relationship goes.
I'd never thought we'd end up here. Sheading
tears over unwasted, wasted years.

I'm on the road where you dissappear,
and the weather just keeps changing here.
Another storm, but it gets better,
cause we're stronger now that we're not together.

All the long walks, the late nights,
Whether we talk or we fight,
telling eachother it'll be alright.
We made eachother smile, but it grew cold,
and the warmth we had didn't have the same
hold.

I'm on the road where you disappear,
and the weather just keeps changing here.
Another storm, but it gets better,
cause we're stronger now when we're not
together.
On the road to a different forever.

# How do you just... (A spoken word poem)

They say take care of yourself and you have to
to take care of everyone else.
The last thing on your mind is your mind, body,
and health.
You are not first.

Yes I do things my way, but to an extent.
When others depend on you there's no time to
wash away the sin, no time to repent. You have
to keep going even if you're skinned alive.
They say time is money, but is it money well
spent?
How do you just...

What do you do when your world's crashing
down and seem like noone's around? Surrounded
by people, but noone can help. Trapped in
circumstances and self-doubt.
A victim effected by cause, and a couple of bad
choices.
Driving nowhere on the road your told leads to
success...
How do you just?

Break away from everything and try not to
drown while everything is pulling you down.
Trying to capsize you before you even touch the
answer.
Fingertips reaching for everything and nothing.
Raching for something but they drown.
The whole world wants you to succeed, or so
they say, but they're not the ones holding you
down.
So how do you just?

# A Cup Never Empty

They say you can't pour from a cup that's empty.
Let me ask you this,
How do you keep giving if there's nothing left to
give?
Keep going without a destination or a home.
Your will, drive and desire act as fule.
Would you consider these things obsolette?
Then how can you be empty?
They say you can't pour from a cup that's empty.
What if we have had it all wrong?
What if we are the cup all along.
You are not empty even though you may feel
that way.
Each time you decide to keep going, you get up
every day.
We cannot see the way others do, but what we
view as empty, they have a whole other point of
view.

# She is a Sunflower

She is a sunflower, but she doesn't know it.
A seed, in a way, part of her is planted in
everyone she meets.
Young and vibrant,
so full of laughter.
You'll want to laugh too.
Soaking up all the bad.
Alone, but still with you.
A root of stability,
constantly growing.
Closed off she may seem, but she will bloom.
Open and bright like sunshine.
Yes, there are days when she is not as bright.
She will wilt.
She will have off days,
but she will still leave a trace of herself on all
who are around.
After awhile she will be better and shine again.
Over and over she gives and gives.
She doesnt see herself the way everyone else
does.
She is a sunflower.

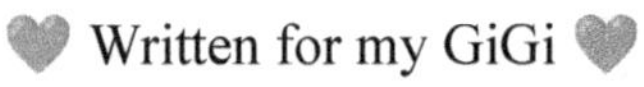 Written for my GiGi

# Panic Attack

You never think your whole life can change in
an instant till it happens to you.
That defining moment of what do I do?
Panic attack,
as you're dragged down by your thoughts.
Don't forget that it's not all bad,
You're moving forward,
But I know it doesn't feel that way.
This is the beginning,
not the end!
My friend, its okay to be scared.
A new chapter and you weren't prepared.
Keep going, you are so much stronger than you
think,
stronger than you seem,
just don't forget to breath.

# Always, Laundry.

This never ending cycle,
Light to dark,
dark to light.
Always plenty more to come, colors, patterns
plain and simple or a variety of fun.
Diffent sizes and weights, occasionally whites
too.
Always so much to do.
Pieces big and small, every size we'll sort them
all.
Every item will have a place,
Always there, folded or unfolded,
clean or dirty
Always, Laundry.

# Overwhelmed

When a certain emotion takes over your whole
body,
It's hard to think.
Hard to act,
hard to speak.
You try to pull away,
but different emotions
all try to surface.
It's hard to focus on just one.
Every second seems longer then the second
before.
It's hard to process,
you become overburdened,
subjected by emotion.

# Best Version of Me

I have cried my eyes out, no doubt
but I won't be down long.
I know, I must be strong,
so I'll get up and go on.
Be the best version of me I can be.
I have little hands and little feet that depend on
me.
Little eyes and ears always observing.
I want to be worthy when they tell someone they
look up to me.
Be the best version of me I can be.
It's not easy when you feel like your drowning.
It's my duty as a mother not to let them
drown with me.
Better evey day, or so I hope.
One day they'll look up and see I'm the best
version of me.

# Normal to Me

I thought things were normal.
Then you came along and showed me a different
perspective.
My eyes were always open,
but now they can actually see.
Until I started to look deeper,
questioning everything.
My mind always knew,
but I chose to overlook.
blinded at first,
but then the truth started to surface.
I thought things were normal.
Only now am I realizing, it was just normal to
me.

# Feeling Inadequate

Feeling inadequate,
It's pretty self explained.
However I'll elaborate,
so we're on the same page.
This insignificant feeling,
always dealing.
As if I lack a purpose, or I am not enough.
I do not see colors as bright as they may be,
or get swept up in a moment.
This doesnt make me not okay,
I just feel like ever day could be a better day.
I myself, could alway be better in some way.
It's pretty self explained.
Feeling inadequate.

# Routine

Do you ever get tired
of the same old grind?
Waking up each morning
with the same thoughts on your mind?
Every day blending into the next?
It's never-ending.

You long for something new.
A break from the norm,
But even when it arises.
The dullness of your days.
The repetition of tasks.
It's like a never-ending chain.

You've been here before.
It all feels so familiar.
The same old conversations.
No one's keeping score.
But you know deep inside,
you're longing for more.

How long will this last?
When will it finally end?
The sameness of it all
is suffocating

But for now, you soldier on
through the daily grind.
Doing what you must do.
Hoping for a change
to break the monotony
of this never-ending chain

The spark of excitement long faded,
Replaced by a numbing cycle.
Dreams and goals become jaded.
Life's too valuable to be stuck in a loop,
a never-ending routine.

# Exhaustion

This feeling of tired.
I just can't shake.
No matter how much I sleep or stay awake.
Always tired, that seems to be my fate.
There are days that are better,
There are days that are worse;
but on the days that I'm not tired,
always feels like a first.
They're few and far between.
Destined to be tired, or so it seems.

# Yin and Yang

Embrace both joy and sadness.
Hand in hand, they are intertwined.
They take turns dancing in the spotlight.
Without the weight of sorrow, would our smiles
hold any meaning?
Happy by default,
Is it even happy at all?
Or more likely a facade to hide how we feel.
Somedays joy is stronger and leads the way.
Other day's sadness is In charge and that's okay.
The yin and yang of life.
We can't appreciate the darkness without the
light.

# Jam Curry

17

A decadent taste you long to eat,
wanting to savor something sweet.
Berries so ripe and ready to share.
Be patient and wait.
Alone or together, it will be just as sweet.
Wait too long and it will wither away,
start to rot, start to fade.
Eat too much and you'll grow to distaste it.
Enjoy it while you have it and do not waste it.
Indulge in the sweetness of each day, embrace it.
For tomorrow may be bitter.
Celebrate today, even if it's fleeting.
Celebrate today, no matter what you're eating.

# Yesterday

Feelings fade, you drift away.
We weren't as close as yesterday.
Time goes by, things seem strange.
All we know is about to change.
This love we have, it was never wrong.
Our feelings are not as strong.
Afraid to let go, scared to hold tight.
Wondering, if it's worth the risk to fight.
We have given up little, yet so much.
Is it so wrong to miss your touch?
Sometime I feel like we should restart with "Hi",
because I never really wanted to say "Goodbye."
Feelings fade, you drift away. We weren't as
close as yesterday.

# Color of Freedom

I hear chains clink and drag behind me,
but the sounds are only in my head.
Everybody thinks I am free.
It is inside where I am bounded and trapped.
Everyone else sees only the outside,
A dove, a light, and a flag.
Beautiful, bright and free,
but they are all blood red through my eyes.
Most people do not see like I do.
I know the road to victory has not one, or four,
but many colors.
Others have seen these colors and live among
them.
Freedom is not a blood bath nor a massacre.
Those already free, know this, for a fact.
I hear facts and truth, they are ahead of me.
The hope of freedom,
strong within my heart.

# Emotional Fire

I watch these flames burn away everything that
resembles you.
So glad, the last of you is gone and we are
finally through.
Yes, I did this once before, for a man who wasn't
you.
Well I was wrong, but now I've seen all you put
me through.
I've never felt tears of joy when I cried over him.
Crying over you, I cry tears of happiness.
I am free from you and your games.
More importantly my heart is no longer your toy.
They say when you play with fire you get
burned,
if only your stuff had a voodoo connection to
you.
You've been playing with fire like a fool for far
too long.
How does it feel now that you're burning and
I'm gone?
It hurts, I know, but it's supposed to.
I hope you've learned, because for you, I am
beyond saving.
Start again, start new, I want to say I wish you
luck, but it isn't true.

Now I have to rekindle old flames, the one you
convinced me to put out.
Honestly, we're both going to be happier this
way,
without each other, for this I have no doubt.

# I am from

I am from warm springs and summers.
Very chilly falls, and winters
that are cold, cold and harsh.
Pine trees, and evergreens,
Sunflowers, and roses.

I am from clothes pins and dog bones.
The old rubber tire swing, the rotting peaches
and vines of wine grapes.
The left out toys, bikes, and tools.

I am from buckeyes
and toys laying about.
From "Boy pipe down"
and "pipe down girl",
Grandma Kathy and her butterflies

I am from mom's homemade ham
and her desserts,
her chocolate chip cookies,
pineapple upside down cake
and her ice-cream.
That is where I'm from.

# My kind of Charming

I keep telling myself;
Wake up, wake up, but my eyes won't open. I
swear that I'm dreaming,
so I close my eyes and count to three,
but you're still standing next to me.
I checked my pulse,
but it isn't fleeting.
You have me second guessing
you're real,
But i know what I'm seeing.
It's the feelings i'm having trouble believing.
You're invading my heart
as if it's never been broken.
You talk to me in ways that leave me unspoken.
I know you're not perfect,
but even when we fight,
I can't believe how all of this feels.
As if it's make-believe and I'm stuck in a dream.
This isn't too good to be true
if I was made for you,
and you're just my kind of charming.

# Happy Ever After

Everyone wants a storybook ending,
but happy ever after isn't always as it seems.
We grow up belive in prince charming.
It isn't easy falling in love.
Even princesses have obstacles to overcome.
Happy ever after doesn't have to be painted
perfect.
We all want someone to have and to hold until
we grow old.
From now on until forever,
however long that may be.
True love is unconditional but not always happy.
It doesn't have to be evething we've ever
dreamed.
Sometimes the perfect dream is in everything we
don't see.
That one person who is evything that make us
believe.
Happy ever after isn't just some crazy dream.

www.ingramcontent.com/pod-product-compliance
Lightning Source LLC
LaVergne TN
LVHW021357200726

843509LV00014B/2891